BEDROOMS

BEDROOMS

A PRACTICAL GUIDE TO DESIGN AND DECOR

EMMA SCATTERGOOD

MEREHURST

First published in 1997 by Merehurst Limited,
Ferry House, 51-57 Lacy Road, Putney, London SW15 1PR

Hardback ISBN 1 85391 547 5
Paperback ISBN 1 85391 603 X

A catalogue record of this book is available from
the British Library

Edited by Cally Law
Designed by Sue Miller
Special photography by Tim Imrie
Styled by Clare Louise Hunt
Illustrated by Susie Morris/Brihton Illustration

Colour separation by P&W Graphics, Singapore
Printed in Italy by Olivotto

ACKNOWLEDGEMENTS
The publisher would like to thank the following photographers and
organisations for their permission to reproduce the photographs listed:

ROBERT HARDING SYNDICATION: page 3 — Simon Brown; pages 4 & 13 —
Fritz Von Der Schulenburg; pages 4 & 51 — Tom Leighton; page 5 —
David Barrett; page 9 — Dominic Blackmore; pages 19 & 33 — Jan
Baldwin; pages 23, 27 & 35 — Christopher Drake; page 35 — Simon
Lee; pages 45 & 50 — Trevor Richards; page 53 — Polly Wreford;
page 59 · Country Homes & Interiors

CAMERA PRESS: pages 1 & 17 — James Merrell; pages 4, 31 & 47 —
Brigitte; pages 6, 15, 25 & 58 — Schöner Wohnen; page 16 — Living;
page 56 — IMS/Sköner Hem

INTERNATIONAL INTERIORS: pages 2, 29 & 55 — Paul Ryan

ELIZABETH WHITING AND ASSOCIATES: pages 40 & 41 — Rodney Hyett

Contents

Introduction

The bedroom should be a retreat, somewhere to relax, to enjoy pleasant dreams and store cherished mementos. It also needs to be a practical place where you can hang clothes, get dressed, put on make-up and prepare to face the day.

In days gone by, the average family may well have made do with a few wool sacks to sleep on, but today we dream of more refined sleeping quarters. Some yearn for romance — a four-poster bed, for instance, complete with beautiful drapes and luxurious linen. Others would choose an almost empty room washed in tranquil shades that allow the soul space to ponder and reflect.

Whatever your dreams, you'll find your inspiration here. These pages are full of sound advice and practical tips for planning the perfect bedroom — even on the smallest budget. You will learn how to transform a small dreary bedroom using just one pot of paint — and how to make the most of any features you are stuck with. There are also ten simple projects for you to enjoy — which will save you yet more money!

Most importantly of all, this book will provide the one vital ingredient for successful decorating — confidence. The confidence to put together not only the perfect bedroom, but to tackle every other room in your house too.

Happy decorating!

Creating a beautiful bedroom need not cost a fortune — in fact the simplest ideas are often the most effective.

Chapter one
Be functional

Right: TV and hi-fi are cleverly concealed behind painted doors in the corner of a bedroom.

When you are planning a new look for your bedroom it can be tempting to dive straight in with the paint-brush or to buy a beautiful suite of new furniture, but try to hold yourself back — for a while at least.

If you want to get really good results, you should go about the redesign of your bedroom in the way a professional interior designer would. And any professional will spend a lot of time discovering how you use the bedroom and what you want from it — before they even glance at their sample book. You should do the same: you want the bedroom to look great but it must be practical too. Everything in it has got to work for you or you will not enjoy spending time there — and after all, you spend at least a third of your life in bed.

This essential planning stage is referred to as 'taking the brief' — in other words, gathering as much information as possible about the room and your needs. In order to do it properly, you will need to arm yourself with a notebook and tape-measure. Then sit down in your bedroom, take a long hard look at it and start to make notes. If you live with anyone else, it is worth asking them for their input at this stage (especially if it is their bedroom you are redesigning) so that there are no arguments later on.

Here are some of the questions you should be asking yourself. If you are planning just a lick of fresh paint and maybe to move the wardrobe from one side of the room to another, this approach may seem excessive, but it really will help you to get the best out of your room. It may even save you from decorating again in just a few months' time.

Who does the room belong to?

This is crucial. You can design your own bedroom as a personal haven — somewhere to unwind and forget the stresses of the day surrounded by personal treasures. A guest bedroom requires a different approach. Although you will want it to reflect your own taste and ideas, it should also appear welcoming and comfortable to whoever comes to stay. A child's room demands yet another set of considerations, with practicality coming top of the list.

Is there any one thing in the bedroom - good or bad - that hits you when you walk through the door?

If so, you should concentrate on minimizing its impact. A good design is well balanced — that is, every element of the room should work in unison with the rest, rather than standing alone. Visitors should walk into your room and comment on how attractive the room is, not say, 'Wow, what a lovely carpet'.

Does the bedroom get much natural light?

If it doesn't, you will need to bear that in mind when it comes to choosing your colour scheme. Most people want to create as much of an impression of light in a bedroom as possible, but if the room is poky and dark and you feel you are fighting a losing battle, you may consider emphasizing the room's more dramatic nature instead. You can afford to be more dramatic in your own bedroom than you would, say, in a guest bedroom, where you want everyone to feel at home.

Are there ways you might make the room lighter?

If your bedroom is in a corner of the house, could you add another window? Or, if you tend to keep your bedroom door closed, would you consider a partly glazed door? (The glass can be stained or frosted if you want to preserve your privacy.) These are decisions that should be made now — you don't want to start knocking down walls after you have laid the carpet.

Which way does the bedroom face?

If you are a morning person, you will appreciate a bedroom that faces east, so you get the sun streaming in as you wake up. If you like a lie-in and the room faces the same way, you will want to invest in some well-lined curtains. The way a room faces also affects the type of light that a room receives. A north, east or northeast-facing room will receive a colder light than those that face south, west or southwest, and so will need a warmer colour scheme (see Choosing colours and patterns, page 15).

How do you use your bedroom?

Obviously the main function of your bedroom is to be a comfortable place to sleep, but it is likely that you do more than sleep there. You probably also use it as a place to get dressed, put on make-up, read and watch TV, depending upon your lifestyle. Think about all the different ways you use your bedroom and what would help to make that space more practical, as well as stylish. The following questions may point you in the right direction:

Could you benefit from having a sink installed?

If the mornings are always frantic in your house, an extra sink could reduce the pressure on the bathroom, giving you a place to wash, shave or put on make-up in peace. If you have space you could even put in a shower cubicle. A guest bedroom is also an ideal place to install personal washing facilities, and estate agents claim that an en-suite bathroom is one investment that will certainly make your house more saleable — if not more valuable.

Does anyone put on make-up in the bedroom?

If so, they will want a mirror that is well provided with both natural and artificial light. Remember that you are likely to use electrical equipment such as a shaver and a hair dryer in front of the mirror, so you will need appropriate sockets sited in the vicinity.

Are there enough mirrors in the room?

If two people are getting dressed in the same bedroom it is worth having more than one mirror. The combination of a wall-mounted small mirror and a full-length mirror works well.

Do you watch television in bed?

It will need to be positioned appropriately, bearing in mind how light will reflect off the screen. Do you have a power point and aerial socket in the right places?

Is the lighting adequate?

Bedside lights are essential, and you could adapt the wiring now so that one switch by your bed controls the various lights and lamps around the room. If you share the bedroom, does one person like to read while another goes to sleep? If so, you might consider a bedside lamp which can direct light on to a book without casting a glare around the room (see Lighting your bedroom, on page 30).

Do you have enough storage space?

If you rely heavily on under-bed storage space, an elegant iron bedstead will be out of the question. Is there room to incorporate more expansive built-in wardrobes, or is there an alcove you could use as a storage area. (Turn to the projects at the back of the book for tips on how to do this, and how to turn a simple shelving unit into something more attractive.) Maybe you have an adjacent spare bedroom that could be adapted into a dressing room.

Is the bedroom also a workspace?

Guest rooms are most likely to have a dual function and need to be carefully designed — especially their storage space, as you will need to pack away your things whenever anyone comes to stay. A table can act as both desk and dressing-table and a wardrobe can double as a filing cabinet.

What is your budget?

Before you go to the shops, you need to fix a top figure — then take off 10 per cent to cover unplanned expenditures. Once you know how much you can afford to spend, it is up to you to juggle the budget. If you have set your heart on a designer wallpaper, that's fine, but you may have to make do with cheaper curtains and bedlinen.

When you start to shop for furniture and furnishings keep a

note of the price of everything, then before you spend a penny add it all up. It is the only way to keep within your means.

You may want to start a notebook for all your plans, perhaps with a folder for brochures and invoices. It will be useful for checking details in the future and an interesting reminder in years to come.

Above: If space is short, make the most of every inch for useful storage areas — without sacrificing style.

Chapter two

Turning problems into solutions

Even if this is your first home, it is unlikely that you will be in the enviable position of starting completely from scratch, able to buy everything you want brand new. Most of us have to accept that, for a while at least, we will have to live with an old bed, a junkshop wardrobe or an ancient carpet.

We also have to live with the existing structure of the house and any problems that may present. Unless you have an unlimited budget, knocking down walls, raising ceilings and putting in new windows will be out of the question. Even if money were no object, structural alterations are not always advisable — a house soon loses its original character if it falls victim to every owner's whims.

Do not despair. With just a few clever decorating tricks and a little confidence you can conceal a lot of the features you are unhappy with and make the most of others — without spending a fortune or calling in the builders. In fact, some of the most challenging rooms turn out to be the most successful in the end.

Making the most of existing furnishings

If you have already worked out your budget for your bedroom redesign, you will have an idea of what you can afford to replace and what you will have to live with for a while. However, if the prospect of living with the old carpet is just too much to bear, look at your priorities again — maybe you can cut a few corners elsewhere and ditch the carpet after all.

Look for end-of-season sales — you may find a remnant that fits the bedroom floor perfectly (especially if it is a small room).

Inevitably, however, there will be some inherited horrors that have to stay put — so here's how to make the most of them.

The old bed: When you dream wistfully of an elegant four-poster, being faced with a dingy divan is a bit of a blow. However, there is no reason why you can't transform your existing bed into the one of your dreams — or something close to it at least. The features that give a bed its style and personality are the headboard and the bedlinen — so cast a critical look over the existing bed to see how you can transform these things.

If the headboard has seen better days, take it off. You could replace it with a new one (if you can afford it) or scour a few architectural-salvage companies to see if you can get a bargain antique cast-iron bedstead — they are often cheaper than the reproductions. Another option is to make your own headboard out of MDF and either paint it or cover it in a pretty fabric. Turn to page 49 for instructions.

You don't need a four-poster to enjoy beautiful bed drapes. It is cheap and easy to hang simple drapes from a coronet above your bed. Turn to page 54 for tips on doing just that — or you could cheat and simply staple or Velcro light fabric drapes to a piece of board above the bed.

If you still hanker after a proper four-poster, take a look at bed frames instead. These are made to fit around your existing divan and cost a fraction of the price of the real thing.

Now turn to the bedlinen. Covering your bed with an assortment of scatter cushions is an instant way of giving your bed a face lift, but if more serious measures are needed, you could make or buy a new duvet cover or bedspread and some smart pillowcases. There is no need to spend a fortune. Plain sets of bedlinen are the cheapest on the market, but can look really special when trimmed with ties or buttons, decorated with fabric paints or edged with a pretty frill (see page 44).

The dreadful carpet:
If you are faced with a carpet that has seen better days, you

A pot of paint can work wonders. Though not everyone is capable of creating a clever trompe-l'oeil mural such as this one, the painted and distressed chest is something anyone could achieve.

may have to think twice before ripping it up. If the problem is simply a few bare patches, try rearranging your furniture to cover the worst of them, and investing in a rug or two to position strategically. If the carpet is simply not to your taste, you could buy a cheap rug large enough to cover the majority of it and then site your furniture over the rest.

Check the state of the floor beneath the old carpet. If you are lucky, you may discover some perfect floorboards or parquet just waiting to be renovated. Bare boards look smart as well as being hardwearing and cheap. You can either protect them with a coat of varnish or give them a stencilled or limed finish (see page 39). Simply add a rug at the bedside to provide a comfortable landing when you get up in the morning.

Ugly furniture: Plain, shabby and cheap pieces of furniture can be transformed into something quite special with just a little time and attention. Take another look at that old wardrobe. Could the handles or feet be changed? How would it look if the paint or varnish were stripped off and restored? Perhaps it could be painted or stencilled to match your colour scheme. (Turn to the project on page 52 to find out how to lime a bedside table, or to the one on page 57 for how to paint a chest of drawers.)

Deceiving the eye

Everyone has their own idea of the perfect bedroom. Some people dream of a large airy space, while others prefer small proportions and sloping ceilings. You may not be able to change the actual structure of your bedroom but you can certainly alter the impression the room gives by emphasizing certain aspects and concealing others. Here are some solutions to common problems:

Ceilings: Too little attention is given to ceilings. We spend weeks deliberating over the walls, floors and furniture, then simply slap a bit of white emulsion up above it all. Yet the height of your ceiling or, more accurately, the perceived height of your ceiling, can alter the whole feel of a room. By using colour cleverly, you can make a startling difference to that perception.

Making it lower: A bedroom should make you feel relaxed and warm, but it probably won't if the ceiling appears cold and high. Make the ceiling appear to be lower by painting it a deeper or warmer shade than the walls. You could even use a patterned paper such as Anaglypta. Add a picture rail and extend the ceiling colour down to the rail for extra effect, and perhaps decorate the walls in horizontal stripes to emphasize the width of the room rather than the height.

Making it higher: In modern houses or tiny cottages the opposite problem is often the case. In a cottage you may want to emphasize the quaint low ceilings by continuing the paint or wallpaper up and over them. Or you may want to make the ceiling recede and appear higher, in which case you could settle for white. Try using a pale pastel shade, lighter than the walls, to acheive the same receding effect.

You can also use pattern to achieve advancing and receding effects: vertical stripes will emphasize the height of the walls and appear to lift the ceiling away from you.

Making it larger: You can fool the eye into thinking that a room is larger than it is by choosing light shades for the walls and furnishings and by using small patterns.

The scale of furniture in the bedroom will also alter your perception of available space. A four-poster bed is a bad choice if you want a room to look larger. Look instead for a lower bed, such as a futon, and slim built-in wardrobes, making the most of any alcove space. Allow the eye to travel over the furniture and prevent any one piece from overpowering the room. Fitted carpet in a pale plain design will naturally draw the eye to the corners of the floor and create an impression of space.

Bold colours and patterns are cleverly combined by taking warm red and introducing flashes of blue from the opposite side of the colour wheel.

Chapter three
Choosing colours and patterns

You can buy the most beautifully designed furniture and furnishings for your bedroom, but if you lack confidence and skill when it comes to colour matching, the finished result will still lack something. Ask people what they find most difficult about interior design and the answer is likely to be colour.

Deciding on a scheme, choosing which colours go with which and then putting together samples can be a daunting prospect. However, current trends in interiors are encouraging us to be bold and to go for splashes of blues, sunflower yellows and even lime green. So how can you put together a successful colour scheme for your bedroom?

Forget the particular colour conundrums your bedroom is posing for a few minutes, and take a wider view. Some people are said to have a good eye for colour — and maybe they have — but that does not mean that colour skill can't be learned. In fact, just a little basic colour theory will take you a long way. It may sound far removed from the immediate problem of choosing a wallpaper to go with your carpet, but if you understand how colours work in theory, it will make every decision a lot easier in practice.

The colour wheel
This is a basic way of demonstrating how combinations of certain colours produce other colours (red and blue produce purple, for example). The wheel becomes more useful to interior designers when you learn that it can be divided into halves — one half comprising all the warm colours (red, red/orange, orange, yellow/orange and yellow, and their various tints and shades) and the other the cool colours (green, blue/green, blue and blue/violet, and their tints and shades). The warm colours are also known as advancing colours, as they have the effect of appearing to be closer to you than the cooler colours on the other side of the wheel, which appear to recede.

Putting theory into practice
You can use the warm side of the colour wheel to warm a bedroom, and the cool colours to make it appear bigger and airier. Remember though that the darker shades of any colour, including green and blue, will make your bedroom appear smaller than a pastel shade. Try not to let the size of your bedroom put you off the darker shades completely. Even a small bedroom can look dramatic in a deep blue.

Think about the kind of effect you want to achieve in the bedroom. The type of person using the room should be your first consideration. For a child's bedroom, bright primary colours are lively, fun and more stimulating than the traditional pastel pinks and blues.

For a guest room, a universally appealing colour such as blue would work well in a room that faces south or west and so gets a warm light — especially when teamed with warm yellow.

In your own bedroom you are free to indulge your fancies. For traditional impact go for deep-red walls — but nothing too bright or it will be so stimulating you won't be able to sleep.

Different colours have been proven to produce certain psychological effects. Blue is the colour of harmony and peace, and so is perfect for a tranquil bedroom. Yellow is a more joyful colour associated with creative energy and power. Rich shades of violet and mauve are reminiscent of church pageantry and inspire meditative thought. Pink is suggestive of passion and caring.

Although some colour schemes use just one colour and then accessorize it with various tints and shades of the same hue, most schemes incorporate an accent colour picked from the opposite side of the colour wheel. If you fancy a romantic pink bedroom, add touches of cool blue or green to balance the warmth. By restricting accent colours to bedlinen and perhaps lampshades, it is cheap and easy to change the mood of your bedroom occasionally.

Incorporating existing furnishings

It can actually help to have existing furnishings that need to be incorporated into the scheme. If it is your old carpet that can't be replaced, decide whether you would like it to play a large or small part in your new colour scheme. If it is a colour you are not fond of, take your main colour from the opposite side of the colour wheel and use the carpet just as an accent. If you decide to use it as the major colour in the room, then look for paint or wallpaper in a similar shade and select an accent colour — or two — from the opposite side of the colour wheel.

If your existing carpet, curtains or bedspread incorporates several different colours, you are lucky — your colour scheming has been done for you. Pick one hue as your main colour to use on the walls and use the others as accent colours.

Staying neutral

Neutral shades such as cream, grey and especially white are extremely versatile and can be used as an extra accent colour in almost any colour scheme. (Black is also regarded as a neu-

By using various shades of coffee and cream, and by introducing pattern, this neutral colour scheme is made as exciting as any bold one.

tral colour, but it can be harsh and should be used sparingly.) You could create a bedroom scheme from neutral shades alone — the trick is to extend the range of shades beyond white to cream, ochre, coffee and maybe degrees of grey. Then use pattern and texture for extra interest.

Making colour work

Colour and pattern can be used to emphasize architectural features and even to define different areas within the room. Alcoves, window frames or the wall behind your bed can all be treated in a deeper or contrasting shade, and areas with dedicated functions such as washing or studying can also be defined with different colours.

Starting points

To get inspiration, flick through specialist homes books and magazines. If a particular bedroom appeals to you, take a closer look at the individual elements in the room and ask yourself what exactly it is that you like. Is it the colour scheme, the layout of the room, the window dressings or the style of the furnishings? You may not be able to replicate that room exactly in your own home (and it would be rather unimaginative to do so), but you can still take inspiration from the overall look.

Why not begin to put together a collection of pictures that appeal to you — perhaps in your bedroom notebook? After a while, you may notice the same looks and themes appearing time and again and it will become clearer what your preferences are.

A bit of history

A common starting point is to take a period in history. The advantage of using historical references is that they never date — a bedroom with a classic wrought-iron bed and a traditional wardrobe will look good for years to come and can be brought more up to date with a few contemporary accessories.

Check what year your house was built. If it is Victorian or

Chapter four

Taking a theme

A simple trick to make your bedroom redesign easier and more successful is to give the room a theme. You can take something as simple as a colour for your theme — or you could be more adventurous and choose a subject such as the night sky and use fabrics, wallpapers and stencils featuring moons or stars. You can keep the theme's influence as subtle as you like — it will still add cohesion to the room's finished look and help with decision-making.

Edwardian, a cast-iron bedstead is the perfect choice. Team it with deep colours, patterned wallpaper, floor-length curtains and heavy furniture for a high-Victorian look, or go for bare

Simple bedroom furniture, traditional bedlinen and a sampler on the wall combine to create a classic Shaker look.

boards, white-washed walls and stripped-pine furniture for a simpler look of the same era. Add accessories such as a bowl and pitcher on your dressing table, and dress bedside tables with floor-length skirts.

A luxurious Tudor look is best-suited to larger rooms. Carved four-poster beds take up a lot of space, which most modern bedrooms don't have. However you could always go for a smaller bed and accessorize the room with tapestry fabrics, heavy wooden chairs and a carved oak blanket chest.

Don't feel left out if you live in a 1960s semi. Rules are made to be broken, and there is no reason why you shouldn't create the look of another era in your home. You could even take a different period in history for every bedroom in the house. Once you have lived in your new home for a while you will develop a stronger feel of what sort of designs are most sympathetic to the house itself.

Movements of influence

Our generation is not the first to break design rules. Throughout history there have been groups of people and influential individuals who reacted against the mainstream designs of their time and produced something refreshingly different. William Morris, for example, inspired the 19th-century Arts and Crafts movement

which moved away from typical Victorian design in favour of a more medieval look. The Shaker community of 19th-century America produced beautiful simple furniture in line with its religious ethics and quite different to mainstream designs. These are just two styles to draw inspiration from, and they are both good starting points for any bedroom theme.

Wish you were here?

Holidays abroad can provide not only happy memories but a wealth of new design ideas based on the interiors of other cultures. Many countries use colours in a different way from the British and evolve their own fashions in interior designs based primarily on the demands of their climate.

In a hot country, a simple bedroom with white-washed or brightly coloured walls, bare tiled floor and simple wooden chairs can look stunning. Remember though that the light here is different from that of the Mediterranean and plain white does not have the same vibrancy in an English bedroom — nor is a tiled floor quite as welcoming on a damp rainy day. Instead of recreating the whole look, steal facets of it and bring home accessories to decorate your sunniest bedroom.

If you've got it, use it

Who knows, the inspiration for your theme may already be in

If cash is scarce but you yearn for grandeur, take 'shabby chic' as your theme and make the most out of what you've got. Plenty of remnant fabric, used in a grand manner, witll help you achieve the look.

your bedroom. A vase of pink gerberas could set you on track for a pink and green bedroom with a daisy theme. Or perhaps you have a stripped-pine chest of drawers to guide you towards a Victorian country look, with colour-washed walls and pretty sprigged fabrics. Or maybe there are some simple tab-headed curtains just crying out to be united with similarly simple Shaker furniture.

Your inspiration might even come from something as insignificant as a china plate hanging on the wall which exudes a certain feel or suggests a new colour scheme. Open your eyes to what you already have around you and what others have done before. Some may call it cheating, but others call it a sense of style!

Let it grow

If you are still lacking in ideas, don't force it. Live with your bedroom for a while and you'll get more of a feel for it. Don't feel you have to pick a theme, then go out and buy anything you see with a daisy on it all in one go. Your bedroom will have more personality if it is allowed to develop naturally over a period of time.

Chapter five

Putting it all together

Once you have some idea of the look you are after for your new bedroom — when you have chosen the theme and colours you would like — it is time to finalize your decisions and make your ultimate choice of wall covering, floor covering, curtain fabric and so on. Don't panic — these may be the hardest decisions you will have to make, but by using a few tricks of the trade you will get a truly professional finish.

Collecting samples

In order to see if the colours and patterns you like will actually work together, you need to get hold of samples. Most stores will offer swatches of fabric, but make sure that you get one large enough to show every colour in the design. You may have to buy a small amount of fabric in order to do the job properly. Don't rely on colour cards to judge how the paint will look as it is hard to reproduce colours accurately. Buy tester pots or the smallest tin, and paint a strip of lining paper in your chosen colour.

Keep your samples together and note down the design's name, the manufacturer and any reference number so that you have them to hand for ordering. It will be useful if you also note down the price, the name of the shop, the fabric width and

pattern repeat so you can work out how much you will need and the final cost for your budget book. Keep all this information in a safe place as it will be useful if you need to replace anything at a later date.

Mix and match

Once you have collected all your samples, mix and match them until you find a combination that works well. This takes much of the guess work out of putting colours and patterns together and can prevent you making big mistakes.

Now position your samples in the spaces for which they are intended. Tack a length of wallpaper to the wall or paint some lining paper with your paint tester and do the same. Put your carpet sample on the floor and attach your fabric samples to the bed, armchair, window or

wherever they will be. Fabrics change their colour according to the light they are seen in, so keep the samples in place for at least a week, noting how they look under natural and artificial light and at certain times of day — especially first thing in the morning and late at night, which are probably the times you use your bedroom most.

Making a sample board

The problem with playing with small samples is that you don't get a true indication of how they will look in the room. A delicate wallpaper pattern can become lost once it has been pasted up, and boldly patterned curtains may unexpectedly dominate the entire room.

To avoid this, you need to consider the balance of your colours and designs on a sample board. Use a piece of card as your base and think of it either as your complete bedroom or as a corner of the room where all your furnishing samples come together. Usually the largest expanses of colour or pattern will be the walls and floor, so cover the board with samples of those materials according to their relative space allocation in the room. The next largest samples are likely to be the bedlinen and curtains, so cut or fold these samples to an appropriate size in proportion to the walls

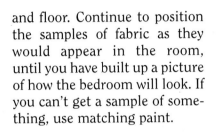

and floor. Continue to position the samples of fabric as they would appear in the room, until you have built up a picture of how the bedroom will look. If you can't get a sample of something, use matching paint.

Once the board is finished, appraise it critically. Does it look as you wanted it to? Is there a good balance of pattern and texture? Play around with your samples until you are happy with the overall look.

Measuring up to the job

You need measurements in order to have a rough idea how much something will cost. A roll of wallpaper might appear to be a bargain until you get home and realize you need 100 rolls. Keep a note of all your measurements (floor area for carpeting, wall area for wallpaper and window sizes for curtains and blinds).

Make a little plan of your bedroom to take around with you too. You do not need to be artistic and it does not even have to be drawn to scale, so long as it indicates all the measurements you need. Draw little sketches of each wall area, or elevation, and mark each measurement on it — from the depth of the skirting to the width of your window frames.

Planning on paper can be useful — and quite fun too. Do some clearly drawn elevations of the room and trace them on to tracing paper. You can then experiment with different ideas, using coloured pens or pencils to add colour. You can soon see how a wall might look with a dado rail added, a mirror hung and so on.

Do a floor plan too and mark on it where your existing power points are, where the radiator is and which way the door opens. All these points are vital, especially when it comes to choosing furniture.

Ready to order
Always check the following points before buying:
- Are all the fabrics suitable for your purposes?
- Do they meet fire-retardant regulations?
- How washable are they? Can they be dry cleaned?
- Are your wallpaper rolls of the same batch number? Order a spare for patching.

Chapter six
Bedroom furniture

A bedroom may not need much in the way of furniture, but the basic pieces it does require — bed, wardrobe and perhaps dressing table — all need to work hard for you. Above everything else, the bed has to be comfortable, the wardrobe needs to be spacious and a dressing table should be practical — but you also want them to look good too. To get the perfect balance of style and practicality within your budget you'll need to do some thorough planning and research — so why not start now!

Before going to the shops, take a good look at what you have already and ascertain whether you do actually need anything else. If you haven't already done so, make sketches of each wall in your bedroom in order to formulate some ideas about how you want the room to look, where your existing furniture could go and what else you may need to buy.

Positioning your furniture

The way you place your furniture can alter the whole effect of the room, making it appear spacious or cluttered, quirky or traditional. Be as imaginative as you can, although it has to be said that an average-sized bedroom offers little flexibility — basically because the pieces you need to juggle are so large. Experiment with a screen, a blanket chest and maybe a circular table to create little areas of interest within the room, and avoid putting every piece of furniture slap up against the wall.

Practical positioning

It is usual to avoid putting the head of a bed directly under a window or up against a radiator (to avoid both draughts and over heating and, in a children's room, to prevent accidents

The right style of bed will give a bedroom its character. A four-poster need not be over-grand, given the right setting.

happening if they jump on the bed). This may eliminate two of your four walls immediately, and if one of the other two has either a fireplace or an awkwardly placed door, you are likely to be left with just one place for your bed.

Remember to leave space for bedside tables. If you want bedside lamps, you'll need conveniently positioned electrical sockets too.

Check that there is room to open wardrobe doors easily, sit comfortably at a dressing table and move in front of a mirror.

Planning on paper

Bedroom furniture is big and heavy, so to avoid straining your back shifting it around the room, do your experimenting on paper first.

Transfer your floor measurements on to squared paper using a scale that allows you to fit your plan on to a sheet of A4 or A3 — 1:20 is normally sufficient. Mark on it your power points, windows, radiators, TV socket and the direction the door opens. Now measure the width and depth of the furniture which is staying in the room. Adapt the measurements to the same scale and cut them out of squared paper. Label each piece and move them around until you get an arrangement that works. Then trace your plan, complete with positioned furniture, on to tracing paper

and put it to one side. You may do several such tracings, but you can compare them more easily if they are all in front of you at once.

Choosing a bed

The only way to decide what sort of bed will suit you is to actually lie on it in the shop. Ideally, experiment with different bases and mattresses until you find a combination that feels right.

Mattresses

There are two basic types of mattress — those with a spring interior and those made of only foam, fibre or latex. You will probably be considering spring mattresses, and these are also divided into two types — pocket spring and open spring. Pocket springs are housed in little fabric pockets that move independently so that your body gets support where it needs it. They are generally more expensive than open-spring mattresses, which vary tremendously according to the number of springs used and the gauge of the wire.

Choosing a wardrobe

If you are a clothes addict it is unlikely that a traditional freestanding wardrobe is going to offer you adequate storage space unless you have a dressing room elsewhere or create extra wardrobe space from an alcove (see page 46). Attractive though they are, traditionally styled wardrobes are quite

Everyone needs plenty of storage space to hide away clutter. Look for a design that makes the most of your available space.

small. If you are renovating an old wardrobe, you may be able to fit two hanging rails running from front to back inside the wardrobe, rather than one from side to side, in order to provide more hanging space.

For maximum storage space, the only sensible option is to have fitted wardrobes installed. These can be designed to your own specifications and will even offer room for suitcases, hat boxes and evening dresses — they are also great for minimizing clutter around your bedroom. The most sophisticated designs can open up to reveal dressing tables and televisions — all cunningly concealed behind a streamlined finish.

If the mention of fitted wardrobes only evokes disturbing memories of Formica and melamine, think again. Fitted wardrobes today can be made to look as traditional or as contemporary as you like, and can be decorated with a range of paint finishes to complement your bedroom scheme.

Chapter seven

Curtains, blinds and drapes

Window dressings set the seal on the look of your bedroom, and indeed on the look of your home, as their style will dictate the impression the house gives from the street.

Style and practicality are both important considerations in your choice of window dressings. If you like to wake up with the sun streaming into your bedroom the last thing you need is heavy and elaborate curtains — unless you are happy to leave them undrawn at all times and simply pull down a sheer blind for a bit of privacy at night. However, if you are someone who likes to lie in until noon, you won't greet the morning sun with the same enthusiasm. Instead, the blackout qualities of whatever you choose will be crucial.

Points to consider

There is a multitude of different window dressings to choose from — which makes decision-making difficult. However, if you focus on your own particular needs it will make the process easier.

First of all consider the following points: your window type and what it overlooks, the style or theme of your bedroom and the amount of light the bedroom receives.

The size and design of your windows will rule out certain styles immediately. Swags and tails are rather grand for most bedrooms and will look incongruous against modern picture windows, while slatted blinds do little for tiny cottage casements. Full-length curtains usually need a longer length of window in order to look balanced, and more imposing designs require an equally grand frame.

If you use your bedroom purely as a place to sleep, the amount of natural light that the bedroom receives will be less of an issue than the quality of the artificial lighting you choose. However, you may want to get as much light as possible in order to put on make-up or study — or simply because it makes you feel happier. If your windows are small, or the room does not get much light, full curtains and impressive pelmets will make the bedroom too dark.

Instead, go for simple designs without low pelmets, and use tie-backs to open up the window area. Or you could extend your pole or track beyond the window frame so the curtains do not obscure the glass at all.

If your bedroom overlooks the street, or other houses look in, choose window dressings that offer a degree of optional privacy during the daytime too. A combination of dressings, such as a flat light-filtering blind with curtains works well, and by drawing the blind on sunny days you will protect your furnishings too.

Curtains

These offer privacy, will help to keep you warm at night (especially if they are given a thermal lining) and with a blackout lining will keep the room dark during the day. Curtains finish and soften a bedroom window frame but, because of the amount of fabric they need to look the part, they can add up to be a rather expensive option.

There is a vast selection of headings and styles available, from tab heads for a simple Shaker look and the more conventional pencil pleats, right through to swags, tails, rosettes and shaped pelmets for a traditional feel. Choose the finish to suit your style, or if that is beyond your means, consider a budget option from the selection below.

Blinds

Cheaper than curtains, blinds will also minimize draughts and offer privacy while allowing more control over the amount of light you let into your bedroom during the day. Roman, roller, paper and cane blinds will roll or fold down to protect your room from the sun and other people's eyes, while slatted blinds can also be adjusted to allow more or less daylight to filter through the slats. All of these styles offer a minimalist effect which alone may be too severe for a bedroom, but they can be dressed up with one of the other finishes outlined below. Festoon and Austrian blinds are more luxurious, with ruched fabric and frilled edges, and are ideal for more feminine and fussy bedrooms.

Lace panels

These are a pretty way of allowing light to filter through the bedroom window while simultaneously offering privacy. They are available ready-made in a variety of lengths and make an attractive alternative to conventional nets. Combine them with curtains or a blind for privacy under artificial light and extra warmth.

Shaped pelmets

Enjoying a well-deserved revival, wooden pelmets are now being used in more exciting shapes which can be covered in fabric or painted to match your scheme. Combined with simple curtains, a pelmet can be used to stunning effect, but it can also work well on a small window as a dressing in its own right. Take care over the size of your pelmet though and make sure it suits the scale of your window.

Dress curtains

If you want curtains only to create a frame for a blind and are never likely to close them across the window, you needn't waste money on surplus fabric: simply buy one width or enough to frame the sides of your window adequately. If the curtains are light, you may even be able to dispense with conventional headings too by using a Velcro type of tape instead. One length of the tape is sewn to your curtain and the other is stuck to the window surround, so you can simply 'stick' your curtains up. You can also take them down easily for cleaning!

Cheap and easy

You don't need to spend a fortune on curtain fabric or even to be able to sew in order to dress your windows with flair. Just try some of the following simple ideas for maximum effect from minimum effort:

Curtain clips

Instant curtains with no sewing required! These rings are just like normal curtain rings but with a little clip at the bottom to hold up pieces of fabric, muslin or lace. Ideal for simply styled bedrooms or as a temporary measure.

Curtains can be used to create separate rooms within a room too. Here, the simple tie-top curtains offer privacy while also allowing the sunlight to filter through.

Swag holders

These enable you to produce cheap and informal swagged pelmets — just feed a length of fabric through two of these curled metal brackets, fixed at either side of the top of your frame. The holders make it easy to create rosettes or to let the fabric fall naturally — so you can be as formal or relaxed as you please. Use them alone over a blind or with curtains in a contrasting fabric. They are also good for draping fabric over your bed, with one holder fixed high above the bed and two at bed height on either side.

Chapter eight

Lighting your bedroom

Never underestimate the power of artificial light. At the flick of a switch it can alter the mood and efficiency of your bedroom, transforming it instantly into a more welcoming place, spotlighting areas of interest and providing perfect illumination for reading, sleeping, making up and mixing and matching clothes. You can spend ages choosing fabrics, wallpaper and accessories, but if your lighting is ineffective, your bedroom will appear uninteresting and dull after dark — which is, after all, when you are most often there. Here's how to achieve perfect lighting in your bedroom.

Before you start

Your lighting system should be planned long before you lift a paint-brush as putting in extra power points and fixing additional wall lights inevitably means fiddling with electrical wiring behind the plaster and makes a bit of mess.

Take another look at your 'brief' to remind yourself of what your lighting needs to achieve. A bedroom may require subtle romantic lighting, so think about how you can create it — and how you can adapt the wiring so that all lights can be turned off at the flick of just one switch.

Children might like a night-light, so make sure that there are adequate sockets by their beds for a nightlight in addition to a bedside lamp and maybe a baby monitor too.

Do you like to read while someone sleeps beside you? Or do you have two children sharing a room? If so, you will need to install bedside lights which can be directed on to a page and will not disturb the other person.

If you have a desk in the bedroom you will need to think about the right sort of lighting for that. An adjustable angle light is the best option.

If you have already planned the position of your bedroom furniture on your scaled-paper plan, consider whether you have enough power points for additional lamps in appropriate places. Check that there are power points by your bedside tables, near the television and handy for the mirror where you intend to shave or use a hairdryer. If there aren't, mark on your plan that you need sockets at those points.

Don't restrict yourself to table lamps when you are planning your lighting. There is a wide range of fittings available, each offering a unique style and direction of light. Knowing a little about all these different types will help you make the right choice.

Ceiling lights

The most common light fitting of all, the ceiling light is usually a pendant and shade in the centre of the room. There are many other types of ceiling light to choose from however.

A pendant and shade direct the light mostly downwards and outwards according to the angle of the shade (although a lot of light is also lost through the hole in the top of the shade, sending light up to the ceiling); spotlights allow you to direct light wherever it is needed; recessed downlighters shine a beam of light directly downwards; domed ceiling fittings give a diffuse light around the whole room.

You do not need tablelamps to provide bedside lighting. Smart pendants hanging from a long flex look chic — and can be controlled by a dimmer switch for extra flexibility.

Wall lights

One of the earliest forms of electrical fittings, these are a more subtle source of light than central ceiling fittings and ideal for bedsides where there is no room for a table and lamp.

The more modern wall lights are often uplighters, sending light up across the wall and on to the ceiling. These are useful for adding attractive pools of light, but are not so practical for reading or studying. Picture lights also fit into this category and can be fitted either above or below the painting or object you wish to illuminate.

Table lamps

These are useful for offering general lighting without resorting to the flattening glare of a central ceiling light. They also allow you to control more accurately which areas of the bedroom are lit.

Position table lamps around the room to create warm pools of light by the bed, on a dressing table and on top of chests of drawers or occasional tables. If possible, arrange your wiring so that you can turn on all table lamps at the flick of just one central switch as you walk into the room.

Floor lights

These are less commonly found in the bedroom unless there is an armchair used for reading — in which case a standard shade or a spotlight stand is more suitable than an uplighter.

Candlelight

For creating the perfect romantic atmosphere! Candles are a soft and flexible light source, whether free-standing on a mantelpiece, wall-mounted on a sconce or hung centrally in a chandelier or lantern. Casting a flattering glow around the room, they create an ambience electric light will never match.

Dimmer switches

Counteract the glare of an overhead light by replacing a standard switch with a dimmer. Cheap and easy to install, this will give you greater control over the lighting and is perfect for waking you slowly on a dark morning, casting a gentle light over children at night or creating a soft light at bedtime.

Chapter nine

Bedroom flooring

A bedroom is the one place where you can afford to be a bit more indulgent with your flooring. Of all the rooms in the house, it has to face up to the least traffic. Unless it is a child's room or you are particularly heavy footed or clumsy, the worst it will have to deal with is some barefooted padding about in the morning and evening — and perhaps the occasional spill of breakfast tea.

Hard or soft?

If you are not particularly bothered about putting your foot down on to something soft in the morning and are still undecided about the various merits of carpet and hard flooring, consider the following:

Hard flooring such as tile, parquet or wood-strip will be tough as well as attractive. Wooden flooring is ideal for traditional-style bedrooms, ranging from country or Shaker through to a simple Victorian look. Tiles are a more unusual (and costly) option, but can look elegant or rustic depending on your choice of finish. Remember though that a bottle of perfume or aftershave will shatter if it hits a ceramic floor and your toes may get quite chilly in the winter.

All types of hard flooring will take spills in their stride and act as a usefully neutral foil to furniture and furnishings for years, however many times you decide to change your colour scheme.

Hard flooring is especially useful in children's rooms as most types can be easily wiped down and cope well with even a bit of youthful artwork imposed on them. You will probably feel the need for a rug or two to soften the look, however, and that combined with the cost of the flooring (plus underlay to prevent rugs from slipping) can be rather expensive.

Carpeting on the other hand offers softness and warmth underfoot and a sense of wall-to-wall comfort. Its insulating qualities prevent every footstep from echoing around the house and there is sure to be a carpet that suits your colour scheme and bank balance.

Don't forget to budget for the underlay when you are doing your sums. Underlay increases the life of a carpet, makes it softer to walk on and improves its insulating qualities. Foam-backed carpets are cheaper but usually of inferior quality and their life span is accordingly much shorter.

If you are considering carpet for a child's room, take a look at carpet tiles. These are made of heavy-duty materials and are easy to install and replace if there are accidents and spills but they are available only in a limited range of colours.

Choosing carpet for your room allows you to play with your newly acquired colour theory and create illusions of space and warmth in your bedroom if necessary. Reds, oranges, yellows and browns will have a warming effect, while blues and greens will cool the room.

Plain light-coloured carpet fitted wall-to-wall will make a room appear larger, whereas heavily patterned carpet in darker colours will have the opposite effect, though to a lesser extent. Plain carpet in either light or dark colours will show every stain and piece of fluff; patterns will allow you to get away with more. Take carpet samples home to get an impression of how they will look.

If you are still undecided, consider a third option — natural matting. This is made from vegetable fibres such as sisal, coir, jute and seagrass and is tough and hardwearing while also offering some of the qualities of carpet — especially those varieties which combine the natural fibres with the softness of wool. Although coloured natural flooring is becoming more widely available, it is most popular in natural shades which complement any colour scheme and suit all styles of bedroom apart from the very grand.

If saving money is a priority, check what's underneath your existing carpet. You may be lucky enough to discover forgotten parquet or some decent floorboards which, with a little sanding and a few coats of paint and/or varnish, you could restore to a beautiful finish. (Turn to page 39 for details of how to give floorboards a limed and stencilled finish.) Always check the complete floor before you start sanding as often a small area is beyond repair or covered in concrete.

Continuing the chequered theme on to the flooring, this painted floor is cheap and easy to achieve.

Chapter ten

Accessories

Once you have finished decorating your new-look bedroom, you can begin to add more personal touches — the ornaments, mementos, pictures and photographs that give a room its soul and character. A bedroom is essentially a private place, somewhere to display your most personal treasures — however a guest room or a child's bedroom also needs accessories to bring it to life and add extra interest.

Recognize a theme

If you have chosen a particular theme for your bedroom it is easy to complement it with appropriate accessories. You could finish a simple Victorian bedroom with sepia photographs traditionally framed, a pitcher and washbowl standing on the dressing table and a rag rug to soften bare boards. Complete a Shaker bedroom with a peg rail for dressing gowns and hand-stitched laundry bags, simple candle sconces, a checked bed throw and a wooden rocking chair. Or add interest to a contemporary setting with simply framed modern prints and brightly coloured vases of sunflowers or tulips.

Turn to historical and geographical text books for a wealth of inspirational ideas, and feel free to mix and match from across the years and continents. A skilled designer is someone who can pinpoint what will go with what, yet also break a few rules. Who cares if you put a mosquito net over your bed in a Shaker-style room, or hang an Indian tin mirror over a Victorian washstand? If it looks good, do it — it's your bedroom after all.

Out with the old?

Buying new accessories for your bedroom is fun, but don't do it at the expense of your existing treasures. You may wonder whether they are really worth displaying, but don't be too quick to relegate them to the dustbin. After all, you've spent years amassing them and they have become a bit of your personal history.

Take a fresh look at your existing bits and pieces to see if you can discover a common theme. Maybe you have many bottles of perfume — if so, arrange the most attractive of them together as a small display. Perhaps you have amassed several wall clocks and don't know what to do with them — how about hanging them all together attractively on the wall? They don't have to be ticking all at once, you could even stop them all at a certain time. You could do the same thing with hats, hanging them on artfully arranged pegs. By placing things together, they immediately become a collection and worth a second glance. Group pieces together on a shelf or table, pin them on a pegboard or hang them on the wall.

A place to relax

Make your bedroom appeal to all your senses — not just sight. A room is immediately more appealing if it smells pleasant, if there is agreeable music in the background and if it is comfortable. These details can have as much impact as the colour of your carpet or the design on your wallpaper.

Buy or pick fresh flowers regularly for their scent as much as their visual appeal. Don't worry if you can't arrange them formally — casual displays in a simple jug will still look and smell beautiful. Dried flowers and herbs can be used for their scent too. Hang a bunch of lavender above your bed to guarantee a good night's sleep.

Above and right: Flowers, candles, pretty
pictures and cushions add the perfect finishing
touches to a feminine room.

Position candles around the room for soft romantic light whenever you want it. Scented varieties will fill the room with delicate perfume, or use night-lights in an oil burner to heat beautifully fragranced essential oils such as lavender or ylang ylang. You don't even need candlesticks — little terracotta pots or baskets packed with moss do the job just as well.

Above all, a bedroom should look comfortable. Stimulate the sense of touch with plump cushions on the bed, soft throws draped over the furniture, a thick rug to sink your toes into — and a warm radiator or open fire in winter. You will never want to leave!

Project one

Smart concealed storage

Why display clutter when you can conceal it behind this smart fabric cover? Choose a fabric to complement your bedroom and use it to hide anything from jumpers to box files.

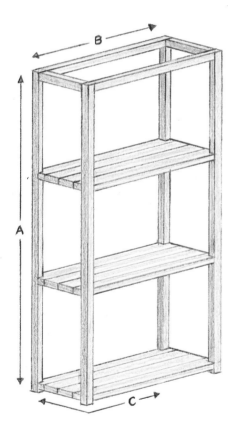

1 Measure up the shelving, taking the height (measurement A), the width (measurement B) and then the depth plus half of the width (B) for measurement C.

2 Cut out the side and back panels. For the back panel: mark out the size of the panel (A by B, plus about 2 cm (¾ in) all round for seams) on to the fabric and cut it out. For the two side panels: mark out the dimensions (A by C, plus about 2 cm (¾ in) all round) on to the fabric and cut it out.

3 Machine stitch the three panels together (right sides of the fabric together) to form one large piece of fabric and hem the raw edges.

4 Measure the width and depth of the top of the shelving and mark out this panel on your fabric. Now mark a line around the panel, 2 cm (¾ in) wider all the way round. Cut the fabric around the outer line, then fold the fabric under along the inner line and press the crease.

Attach the top panel to the rest of the cover using a tacking stitch with the right sides of the fabric together. Place the cover over the frame to check the fit; hand-stitch the panel on and remove the tacking stitches.

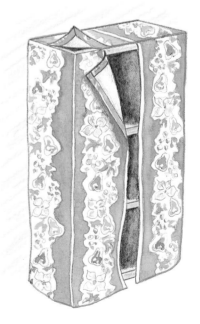

5 To finish the cover I gave it a scalloped edge, but you could equally point the ends, like flags, or square them off. To make scallops, I used a plate as a guide and traced the design on to paper to make a pattern. Check that the paper pattern fits the top of the unit.

Measure around the top of the frame and cut a piece of fabric to that length, plus 2 cm (¾ in) seam allowance, and 46 cm (18 in) wide. Fold the fabric in half, lengthways, with the right sides together.

When I was happy with my paper scallops, we used the paper pattern to mark the design along the length of the fabric.

6 Machine-stitch along the edges of the scallops, then cut out the shapes, a little less than 1 cm (½ in) beyond your stitching. Snip into the seam twice on each scallop to allow it to lie flat without rippling, then turn the scallops the right way out and press them. Hand-stitch them to the edge of the roof panel.

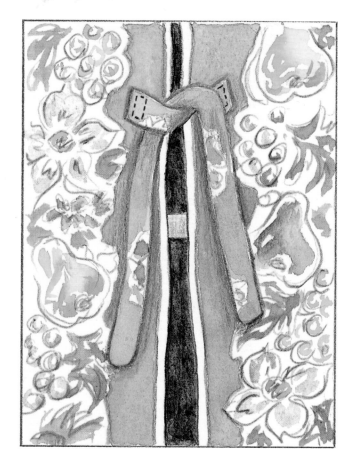

7 Make two or three sets of fabric ties by cutting four strips of fabric, roughly 40 cm (16 in) by 10 cm (4 in) for two sets of ties. Fold each strip in half lengthways, with the right sides together, and stitch the raw edges together. Trim off any excess fabric, turn the ties the right way round and press. Turn the ends in and handstitch them down. Stitch the ties on to the front of the cover.

Project two

Liming a bedroom floor

You will need
- White gloss paint (ideally the sort that only needs one coat)
- White spirit
- A paint can
- A wide paint-brush
- A sponge
- Clear non-yellowing heavy-duty varnish (yacht varnish is ideal)

You don't have to splash out on real limed wood to achieve the same cool and elegant look. By following these easy steps, you can achieve a limed effect with just a pot of white paint and a little white spirit.

1 Prepare the floor boards by vacuuming and cleaning them, then prime them with varnish thinnned with white spirit — you will need to apply two coats, leaving the boards to dry thoroughly between coats.

2 Mix the gloss paint with an equal amount of white spirit in a paint can, then paint it on to the boards with a brush, covering a small area at a time.

3 Before the paint dries, quickly wipe it with a dry sponge to give an uneven and soft limed effect.

4 Protect the floor by sealing it with a couple of coats of heavy-duty varnish.

Variation

To give your floor a more decorative finish, you could stencil the edges of the room, and even decorate the middle too. Choose a stencil with quite a large design, especially if the room is spacious, otherwise it will look lost. Practise stencilling on paper first and position the paper stencil design on the floor to make sure you are happy with the look.

When you start to stencil, use a stencil brush and stencil paint, and keep your brush dry so that the finished look is subtle and almost faded. Use masking tape or spray mount to keep the stencil in place as you work and keep checking it for a build-up of paint so that it does not smudge.

Project three

Papier mâché mirror

You will need

- An old tin tray
- Newspaper torn (not cut) into strips a bit longer than the diameter of the tray
- Wallpaper paste
- A mixing bowl
- Vaseline
- A small mirror, cut to size
- White emulsion paint
- Pencil
- Paints to decorate

With a little ingenuity you can create original accessories for your bedroom that hardly cost a penny. Making things from papier mâché is easy and fun — so start saving your old newspapers now.

1 Smear Vaseline evenly over your tray, including the rim. This will stop the papier mâché from sticking to its mould.

2 Mix up the wallpaper paste or use flour and water. Wipe the paste along the strips of newspaper and lie them across the base of the tray, slightly overlapping and in one direction only. Let the ends of the strips go over the edge of the tray (they are easily trimmed later).

3 When the base of the tray is covered with the first layer of paper, lay a second layer of strips over it in the same manner but so that they lie at right angles to the first layer. Continue to build up layers, in alternate directions, until you have eight layers of newspaper. Put the tray to one side in a warm dry room for a couple of days. Use light weights to ensure the paper does not lift unevenly as it dries.

4 When the frame is dry, it should come away from the mould easily. Take the mirror — cut to a size that suits the frame — and position it on the frame. Draw a line around the

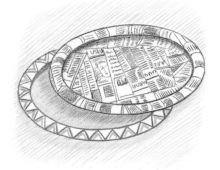

mirror and use that as a guide for the rim. Cover some shorter strips of newspaper with paste and roll them between your hands to form sausages of newspaper. Shape these around the mirror line and leave to dry for a few days.

5 When the rim is secure, give the whole frame a couple of coats of white emulsion. Practise your design ideas on paper, then mark them out on the frame (once it has dried) with pencil.

6 Paint in your design. Acrylic paints are ideal. You can also use the silver and gold foil from sweet papers to decorate the frame.

7 When the frame has dried, you may coat it with a clear non-yellowing varnish if you wish.

8 Buy a small hanging ring and stick it to the back of the mirror.

Project four

Decorating plain pillowcases

Plain pillowcases can be given a new look by simply edging or decorating them. Take your inspiration from the design of your bedroom — for a romantic look choose pretty broderie anglaise, or for something more celestial try your hand at fabric stamping. If you are really adventurous, you could experiment with fabric paint and create a design of your own or one adapted from a pattern from your quilt, your curtains or even a picture on the wall.

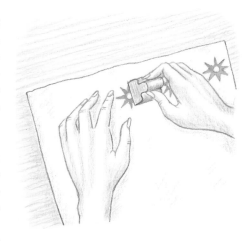

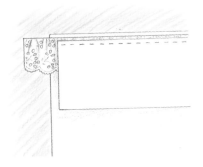

You will need

- Generously sized pillowcases
- A length of broderie anglaise (depending on the size of your pillowcase and the type of trimming you choose)
- Thread to match
- Scissors

Broderie anglaise trimming

1 Measure the complete circumference of your pillowcase. If you are planning on trimming it with broderie anglaise that has already been gathered, you will need to buy this amount, plus a little bit extra for working. If the trim you use is not yet gathered, buy a length of broderie anglaise one and a half times the circumference of the pillowcase to allow for the gathering.

2 If you have bought ungathered broderie anglaise, or a similar edging material, stitch along the raw edge with a loose running stitch and gently gather it along the thread to create a ruffle.

3 Turn your pillowcase inside out and cut off the existing seams as close to the seam as you can, so that you lose as little space in the pillowcase as possible. Cut open the folded edges of the pillowcase too so that every edge is open.

4 Place your gathered trim between the front and back sections of the pillowcase with the broderie anglaise turned inwards to face the centre of the pillowcase. Stitch the side seams together

again, over the edge of the borderie anglaise to attach it. Finally, use a zigzag stitch over the raw edges to neaten them.

5 Turn the pillowcase the right side out and press it.

To stamp a pillowcase

You can buy ready-made stamps and stamp paint from art shops and haberdashery stores, or you could make your own from a potato. Cover

the base of the stamp evenly in paint, using a roller or a sponge, and practise on a similar piece of material, such as a handkerchief, before tackling the pillowcase.

Always recoat the stamp with fresh paint before you make each print and work in such a way that you avoid smudging the prints you have recently done.

Variation

Give your duvet cover a unique finishing touch by adding fabric ties to the opening — they need not replace the existing fastening, simply enhance it. Turn to page 38 for instructions on how to make the fabric ties for the fabric-covered shelves and make up your ties to roughly 12 cm (5 in) long. Once you have made enough pairs, pin them to the edge of your duvet cover at measured intervals to ensure that you have enough and are happy with the look. If your duvet cover is fastened with buttons, position the ties as close to each button or popper as possible. Turn the duvet cover inside out and stitch each tie close to the edge, ensuring that its partner is directly opposite it.

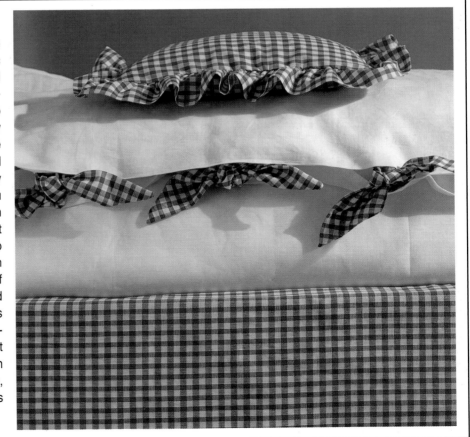

Project five

Making a wardrobe out of an alcove

Many period houses have chimney breasts in the bedrooms with alcoves on either side which can be put to good use as wardrobes — saving both space and money.

1 Choose two suitably sturdy rails with matching brackets — one rail for the curtain and the other for your clothes. If you choose closed circular-end brackets (instead of the open-top designs that a pole can drop into) make sure that the fixing screws are accessible once the rail is in place.

2 Decide where the rails should be positioned. There should be at least the width of a clothes hanger between the rear wall and the curtain rail to ensure that you have enough hanging space. A suitable height for the curtain rail should be in the region of 195 cm (77 in). The clothes rail should be at a convenient height for you to reach — 175 cm (70 in) is standard.

3 Mark the position of the brackets' fixing holes, then drill into the wall to make the screw holes. Fix one end-bracket to the wall and slide in the rail at that end. Now fix the other bracket. Repeat the process for the curtain rail, remembering to put the curtain on to the rail before fixing the second bracket.

You will need
- Measuring tape
- Two support rails
- A drill
- A screwdriver
- Rawl plugs
- 8 x No. 6 1½ in screws
- Fabric for curtains
- Matching thread and needle

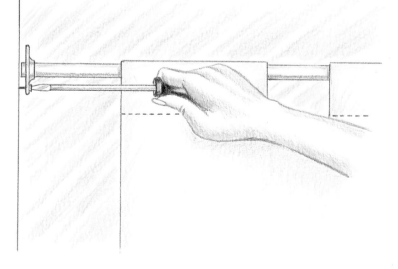

For the curtain

1 Estimate the amount of fabric you will need to make two curtains (or one in a small alcove). Allow extra for working and hems, plus the heading tabs.

2 Hem the side seams and the bottom, then either attach heading tape to the top edge, or make heading tabs for a simple look similar to this one.

3 To make tabs, simply cut out small lengths of material twice the length of your finished tab and twice the width. Fold the strip of material lengthways, right sides facing, and stitch up the long sides. Turn the tabs the right way round, fold them in half and press them. Pin them into position along the top edge of your curtain fabric and stitch them in position. To hide the raw edges, stitch on a facing strip of material at the same time.

Variation

If you haven't got a suitable alcove, you can put a corner to good use by cutting a top and bottom for your wardrobe out of MDF (medium density fibreboard). The curtain rail shown here is curved, which is more difficult to achieve, but you could create a similar effect with a straight rail.

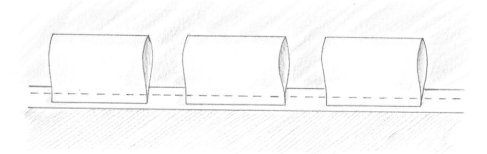

You will need

- Medium density fibreboard or plywood to fit your own specifications
- A sheet of paper as big as the board
- Jigsaw
- Foam rubber (2.5 cm–5 cm/1 in–2 in thick)
- Pencil
- Scissors
- Tape measure
- Glue
- Material for board
- Piping
- Matching thread

Project six

Making a headboard

If you don't like your existing headboard — ditch it! Why not, when it's so easy to make this smart fabric-covered alternative?

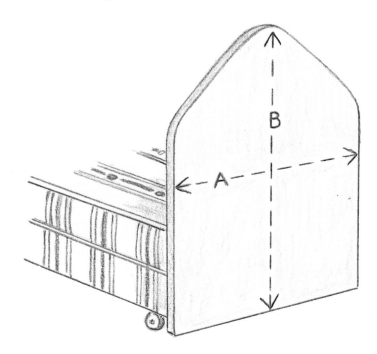

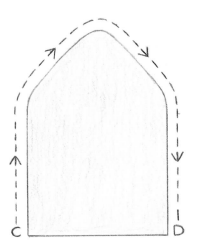

To make the board

1 Measure up for your headboard by taking the width of your bed (A) and the height from the floor to the top of the base of the bed, plus 92 cm/36 in (B).

2 Make a template (paper pattern) of the shape of the headboard to fit your measurements. It's easier if you fold the paper in half width-ways and draw out half of the shape so that when you cut the pattern it is symmetrical. Open out the cut pattern and pin it on to your board, then draw around it with a pencil or chalk. Keep the paper pattern for step 3 and cut out the shape carefully with a jigsaw.

3 Cut the foam to the same shape as the board, using the paper template again as a guide. Then cover the headboard with the foam — using glue to attach it — for added softness and depth.

To make the cover

The cover is made as a slip-over cover, similar to a pillowcase, with an opening along the lower edges.

1 Estimate the amount of fabric you need by measuring the sides and top edges of the board, plus 5 cm (2 in) for working (C to D in diagram). This will also be the measurement for the strip of material that links the two panels. The amount of piping needed will be double this measurement.

2 Cut out two pieces of fabric the size of the headboard plus 1.2 cm (½ in) all round for seams. Cut a strip of fabric to fit around the sides and the top edges of the headboard, plus 2.5 cm (1 in) for seams. Make this strip as deep as the padded headboard plus 2.5 cm (1 in) for seams.

3 Take one of the fabric panels. With the right side facing you, place the piping on top, with the piping facing inwards. On top of the piping, place the gusset strip that has been cut to fit around the sides. With the wrong side of the fabric facing you, pin together and then stitch

Variation

Tatty wooden headboards can be brought up to date with a lick of paint. Use eggshell or gloss paint for a hardwearing finish and sand and prime the wood before you start. If you fancy a complex design, mark it out with pencil before you start and leave the paint to dry well between coats.

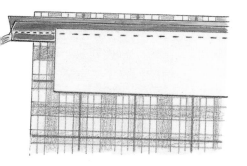

around the sides 1.2 cm (½ in) from the edge to form a flat seam.

4 Trim the corners and the seam allowances to about 6 mm (¼ in) from the stitching.

5 Join the gusset strip and piping to the back section of the cover in the same way and finish.

6 Hem the open edge at the bottom by turning in 1.2 cm (½ in), then turning it again to make a double 6 mm (¼ in) hem.

7 Press the cover and slip it over the headboard.

Project seven

Colour washing

Colour-washed wood has a soft 'aged' look which is perfect for the simple bedroom and easy to achieve. Before you treat any piece of wood in this way you need to remove all existing paint or varnish with an appropriate stripper, then sand it down.

You will need
- A wire brush
- Emulsion paint
- Water
- A wide paint-brush
- A soft lint-free cloth or dry sponge
- Sandpaper
- Clear paste wax

1 After the wood has been prepared, open up the grain by rubbing the piece of furniture with a wire brush. This helps the wood grain to absorb the paint. Always work in the direction of the grain to avoid marking the wood.

Variation
You can achieve a look similar to this chest using liming wax or paste instead. Apply the paste with wire wool in a circular motion then buff it with clear paste wax on a lint-free cloth.

2 Mix the paint with water using about six parts paint, one part water, and test the effect on a small area. Wash the paint roughly over the surface in the direction of the grain, treating just a small area at a time.

3 When the paint is nearly dry, wipe off the excess with a dry sponge or lint-free cloth until you can see the grain of the wood. Next day, sand the surface once more to finish and seal it with a clear paste wax.

Project eight
Elegant bed drapes

It is easy to achieve this smart bed dressing with the help of a bed-canopy kit (available from most good haberdashers) or a semi-circular bracket. The sewing involved is straightforward, so anyone can have a go.

You will need

- A canopy-frame kit (or a semi-circular frame which can be attached to a wall bracket)
- Two widths of fabric, each 452 cm (88½ in) long
- Matching thread
- A screwdriver
- Hooks for curtain tie-backs

1 Fix the wall bracket for the canopy frame approximately 120 cm–150 cm (4 ft–5 ft) above the centre of your bed.

2 Hem the side seams on your curtain material.

3 With the wrong side of the fabric facing you, fold down 6 cm (2½ in) from the top of the curtain. Press along the fold.

Now fold down a further 12 cm (5 in) and press along this fold. This will create a hemmed effect to the fabric channel for the canopy frame.

4 With the wrong side still facing you, machine stitch along the base of the fold. Then machine stitch another row 6 cm (2½ in) above this to make the channel for the canopy frame to fit in.

5 Hem the base of the curtains, either by machine or by hand.

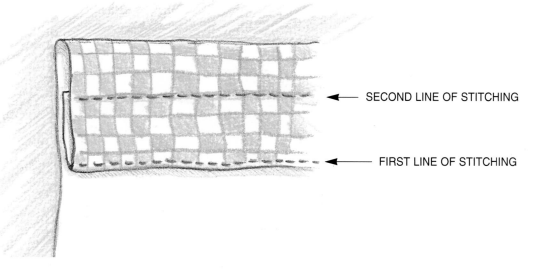

← SECOND LINE OF STITCHING

← FIRST LINE OF STITCHING

6 Slip the curtain along the canopy frame, and smooth the gathers as you go. Close the dovetail on the canopy frame by slotting the two ends together and fit it into the wall plate. You can add extra decorations to the coronet if you wish, by stitching on fabric flowers.

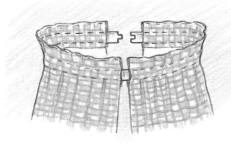

7 Attach the hooks for the curtain tie-backs to the wall on either side of the bed, so that the fabric falls attractively. You can make simple tie-backs by cutting out two pieces of fabric in the shape you want, stitching them with the wrong sides facing, then turning them the right way and stitching on a D-shaped ring at either end of the tie-back. If you want the tie-backs to be quite stiff, use an iron-on or spray fabric stiffener before sewing.

Variation

For a more romantic touch with a hint of the tropics why not go for a mosquito-net design? Lengths of muslin fabric are draped to create the net effect from a specially designed apex ring hung from the ceiling. Here a panel of lace has been added to soften the overall look.

You will need
- Tracing paper
- Medium-hard pencil
- Soft pencil
- Craft knife
- Emulsion paint
- Stencil brush
- Stencil card or acetate

Project nine
Painted chest

There is no need to spend a fortune on new furniture for your bedroom. Even the most uninspiring pieces can be given a new lease of life with a lick of paint and perhaps some new handles. Rummage through your local junk shops and see what you can find — as long as it hasn't got woodworm, you're in business!

There's no need even to buy new stencils to decorate your furniture. Here's how to make a design that is quite unique.

1 If you are not confident of your own artistic skills, you can copy a part of a design from a piece of fabric, a book or even a sheet of wrapping paper to make a stencil. Simply trace it on to tracing paper using a soft pencil.

2 Transfer your traced design on to stencil card or a thin sheet of acetate. Turn the tracing paper over so that the pencil design is on top of the acetate and fix it in place with tape. Take a medium-hard pencil and rub over the pattern so that the pencil tracings on the other side are transfered to the acetate.

3 To cut out your stencil design, lay the card or acetate on a cutting mat and use a craft knife to cut out the design.

4 To help you position your stencil accurately on the furniture, it will help if you use a spirit level. Fix the stencil in position with some low-tack tape and select your paint.

5 Stencils should be subtle, not solid blocks of colour, so only load your stencil brush with a little paint and wipe off any excess. Instead of using conventional brush strokes, 'stipple' the paint over the stencil, using the flat edge of the brush.

Preparation tips

Before painting furniture, you need to prepare it. If it has been waxed or varnished, strip it first, then neutralise it using a mixture of 1:20 vinegar to water. If the wood is new or bare, give it a couple of coats of primer. Repair any damaged pieces with filler, and sand it carefully before painting with an oil-based paint, such as eggshell or gloss.

Project ten

Découpage chest

Découpage is a rather grand-sounding term for something which is in fact very simple. The Victorians were particularly fond of decorating pieces in this way, but as you can see from our little chests, there is no need to work with the rather twee designs that they preferred.

Découpage is perfect for decorating bedroom furniture, be it large or small, and can turn a piece of junk furniture into something spectacular. Start with a small chest such as this, then progress to something larger, such as a blanket box or even a wardrobe!

You will need
- A chest to decorate
- Wood primer
- Emulsion paint
- A pair of small scissors (curved nail scissors are perfect)
- Wrapping paper, photocopied pages from a book or specially prepared découpage pieces (available from stationers and art shops)
- Fine sandpaper
- Clear non-yellowing varnish

1 Prepare your chest by sanding it down. If it is new, give it a coat of wood primer.

2 Give your chest a couple of coats of paint.

3 Carefully cut out your designs from the wrapping paper and start experimenting with positions on the chest. The best way of doing this is by using Blu-tack. Play around until you are completely happy, then stick the pieces down with a small amount of glue. Wipe away any excess that seeps from underneath the paper.

4 When all the pieces are stuck to the chest, leave them to dry before applying the first coat of varnish. The idea is to build up thin layers of varnish until you can no longer feel the difference in levels between the pieces of paper and the chest itself Obvously, the thicker the paper you use the more layers of varnish you will need. Let the varnish dry properly between coats and, after your first couple of coats, lightly sand the chest to get rid of any runs or blobs. You want it as smooth as possible so that it looks as if the design has been painted on. Expect to apply about eight layers of varnish.

Variation

You can use découpage to decorate plain storage boxes too. Hide your clutter under the bed by tidying it away in decorated shoe boxes or cardboard boxes such as these.

Suppliers

Oliver Bonas
801 Fulham Road
London SW6
Tel: 0171 736 8435
Decorating Plain Pillowcases - page 44

Cologne & Cotton
791 Fulham Road
London SW3
Tel: 0171 736 9296
Smart Concealed Storage - page 36
Decorating Plain Pillowcases - page 44

Crucial Trading
77 Westbourne Park Road
London W2
Tel: 0171 229 3465
Smart Concealed Storage - page 36

Damask
3/4 Broxholme House
New Kings Road
London SW6
Tel: 0171 731 3553
Smart Concealed Storage - page 36

Elephant
94 Tottenham Court Road
London W1
Tel: 0171 813 2092
Papier Mâché Mirror - page 42

Jerry's Homestore
163 Fulham Road
London SW3
Tel: 0171 581 0909
Smart Concealed Storage - page 36
Papier Mâché Mirror - page 42
Decorating Plain Pillowcases - page 44

Paperchase
213 Tottenham Court Road
London W1
Tel: 0171 580 8496
Decoupage Chest - page 60

The Pier
200 Tottenham Court Road
London W1
Tel: 0171 637 7001
Smart Concealed Storage - page 36

Index